LOVE
HURTS

By

David Lee Crump

Copyright © Year 2026.

All Rights Reserved by **David Lee Crump.**

No part of this publication may be reproduced in any form, or by any means, electronic or mechanical, including photocopying, recording, or any information browsing, storage, or retrieval system, without permission in writing from David Lee Crump.

ISBN

Hardcover: 979-8-90190-256-1

Paperback: 979-8-90190-255-4

Dedication

This book has been dedicated to my family, friends, and to all those who have been broken before. The ones who have backed me up over the years.

To the ones that are still learning how to deal with love and heartbreak. We have to learn how to pick ourselves up and dust ourselves off.

Acknowledgement

I would like to extend my sincere gratitude to the individuals whose contributions and support played an important role in bringing this book to completion.

My appreciation goes to **Dell Renoud** for the cover art, which thoughtfully captures the essence and tone of this work through creative vision and design. I am also deeply thankful to **Alesia Honor** for her assistance during the writing process, offering support and valuable help along the way.

I would like to acknowledge **Charles Smith and his team** for their support and collaborative efforts.

To everyone who contributed their time, talent, and dedication, thank you for being part of this journey. Your support made this book possible.

About The Author

My name is David Lee Crump, and my book is about heartache and pain and love that I have suffered, and others have suffered over the years. I have heard many stories about people's relationships failing.

I decided to write poems about how I have lost loved ones and the struggles that come with it. I have loved and lost love before.

I wrote these poems to help the suffering and lost souls, letting them know there is hope in everyday things. Love is one of the hardest things you can go through.

Table of Contents

Dedication i

Acknowledgement ii

About The Author iii

Introduction 1

Love Hurts 3

If You Can Do This! 5

Make a Wish for Me 7

My Love Is Real 9

I Miss You So Much 13

The Beautiful Lady Song 15

Can You Make Me Happy? 17

So Hard to Say Goodbye 20

Looking So Good to Me 22

I Cry So Hard 24

I Am Your Heart and Soul 26

You Left Me All Alone Again 28

It Hurts So Much 30

Mom, Don't Cry Anymore 33

I Am a Real Soldier 34

I Miss You Too 36

Until We Meet Again 37

You Are My Queen 39

Introduction

This book is somewhat of a deep dive into people's lives. There are trials, tribulations, a survival guide, and a healing guide. Those who have lost someone they love, and how it feels knowing someone is out there with the same feelings as them.

Love Hurts

If you can fulfill this for me,

Makena's deepest wishes will come alive.

My love remains genuine;

I yearn for you intensely.

The enchanting lady sings her melody.

Can you bring joy to my heart?

If I offer you my devotion,

Parting becomes unbearably difficult.

You appear so captivating to me,

Yet tears flowed profusely from my eyes.

I am your very heart and soul,

Cherishing you, though you abandoned me once more.

The pain is overwhelming.

Please refrain from weeping on my behalf.

Mom, cease your tears now;

I stand as a true warrior.

I long for you as well.

You reign as my queen.

Why have you forsaken me?

If you choose to act,

You've orchestrated it all.

I adore you. Can you stop these cascading tears?

If I pose a question to you, if you are capable...

I ache from missing you deeply;

Why do I bestow my love upon you?

If You Can Do This!

If you can do this one thing for me,
just one,
I will give you my love
and my soul.

Can you do that for me?

I give you pain.
I give you love.
I give you trust.

Will you still hold me
when all of it is heavy?

Can you do this for me?

When I cry,
when my voice breaks,
will you pull me close
and tell me
we will be better together?

Can you do one thing for me?

Let the world see
that I love you.
Not quietly.

Not halfway.
But fully.

Tell them that at the end of our lives
we will still choose each other.

Tell our family.
Tell our friends.

Tell them we are one
that God put together,
and no one has the power
to tear us apart.

Because I will always put
you and me
on the front line first.
I will stand before you.
I will hand you the shield.
I will give you my life
without asking for yours.

I do not ask for much.
Just this, keep my love
alive in your heart.

I will always love you.

Make a Wish for Me

Make a wish for me.
Tell me what you want.

How far do I have to go
just to see you smile?

I would cross lakes.
I would cross rivers.
I would drive through states
with your name in my mouth
and hope in my chest.

I would call your phone
just to say, *hello*.

And wait.

Make a wish for me.
My wish was simple;
you in my arms,
your smile becoming my peace.

Take my world with you.
If you are smiling,
I will be too.

You became my second wind.
My heartbeat when mine felt weak.

Someone turned my dream
into something real.

I thank God for making you.

I walked on cloud nine,
lost in the sky with you,
learning how to breathe
while holding your hand.

I believed we had wings.
I believed love was enough.

And even if my wish
came true only for a moment,

the greatest miracle
is this,

I got to love you.

My Love Is Real

I wake up to the blue sky,
and it reminds me
that I am still breathing.

I step into the yard,
feel the green grass beneath my feet,
and for a moment
I feel steady again.

When the wind moves past me,
it carries your name.
I hear it
even when you are not here.

When I look at you,
I do not just see a sweetheart.
I see someone my heart
refuses to let go of.

My love is real
because I give you everything.
All of me.
Every piece I have left.

I do not know how to love halfway.

I want all of your love too.
I want to be your king,
my queen,
the one who stands with you
when the world turns heavy.

I see it in your eyes.
You are tired of being strong alone.
You want someone
to love you
and not walk away.

I would drive around the world for you.
Not once.
Not twice.
As many times as it takes.

If it rains
and you need someone to cover you,
I will be there.

And if it keeps raining,
and you are still cold,
still hurting,
I will stay.

I will be that person for you.

We will walk in the park,
go to the mall,

sit in dark movie theaters
holding hands
like nothing else matters.

People will see us.
Sweaty, smiling,
walking close.
They will know
we belong together.

Those small moments
mean everything to me.

I will carry my sword and shield,
not to fight you,
but to protect what we have.

I will build a castle around us,
not out of stone,
but out of loyalty,
patience,
and love that does not run.

My love is real
because you helped mend
the parts of me
that cried in silence,
that felt broken,
that did not know how to hope anymore.

The sun keeps rising toward us,
even after the darkest nights.

And every time it does,
my heart remembers.

My love for you
is still real.

I Miss You So Much

I am crying for you now
It hurts so much not to see you
Sad times linger
My world will never be the same

The rain falls
Cold air swirls around me
I remember your beautiful smile
The memory clings to me

I long for your voice
Saying hello, asking how I am
Saying goodbye, take care
You brightened my days
Now I cry and whisper your name

I told you everything once
All the things I loved about you
Now I cannot speak
Because you are gone

I pray to God
That one day we will meet again
My sunshine will return to my life
The tears will finally stop

And I will tell you

Everything I feel

Let the warmth of your love

Return to me once more

The Beautiful Lady Song

If you sang,

I would listen to you sing.

You make me feel so happy,

so alive inside.

I would run through streets and cities,

over mountains, just for you.

The beautiful lady singing her song,

and my heart following the sound.

I would let my guard down for you.

I would listen with my whole soul.

Your world would become mine,

because you made me happy too.

The birds would sing along with you.

Even the dogs would sing love songs.

I would watch the stars

and wish the song would never end.

Your smile, your heartbeat,

singing so sweet and strong.

The blue sky would smile with you,

the sun shining brighter than before.

No one will take me from you,

because my heart belongs only to you.

People will say

we are crazy love birds in the sky.

I belong to you always.

The beautiful lady sings.

I will hold your hand and tell you

you sing so beautifully.

I will tell the world

this love is mine.

Ask anything of me,

I give it freely.

Let my heartbeat move

to one lovely beat for you.

I thank God for you in my life.

This is my true love for you.

Can You Make Me Happy?

Sometimes, I walk alone,

asking my own heart a question:

Can you make me happy?

I want to give you all I have,

every piece of love inside me,

my world, and even more.

I see no one else,

only you in my life.

My heart hurts,

my eyes cry so hard.

My love feels low,

pressed down by fear.

Still, I ask:

Can you make me happy?

I would give you anything,

just to see your smile.

I would work so hard for you,

my queen, you are to me.

No one could ever say

I do not love you;

I would show it every day.

A love like mine is hard to find.
You are always first in my heart.
Day and night, everywhere we go,
my love would show.
My heart would beat with yours,
my world shaped by your words,
until the end of time.

The sun would smile on us,
the clouds would stay blue and clean.
If you can do that part for me...

I will always be in love with you,
if I give you my love.

But tell me:
What word would you say to me?
What would you show me?
What would love become?

If I give you my love,
will you leave me alone?
Will you tell others how weak I was?
Will you hurt me, day and night?
Will you turn my love to dirt,
cut it apart, and throw it away?

Will you burn my words,

pour cold pain through my heart,

and let it run like ice through a stream,

if I give you my love?

Or will you change me

into someone new,

falling in love with you

for the first time again?

I hope we walk together in the park,

roses lining the trees,

love growing with every step.

I hope my love makes you softer,

teaches you how to love.

An angel would dance around us,

and the world would breathe and say:

Yes, you have won.

Love and joy have returned again.

So Hard to Say Goodbye

It is so hard to say goodbye,

because the tears run down my face.

My heart breaks every time I try,

and still, I say your name.

The wind is blowing, calling you.

I hear you everywhere I go.

The ocean is not deep enough

to hold the tears, I see in your eyes.

It is so hard to say goodbye.

I would climb the highest mountain

just to call your name again.

The whole world can see

the broken heart I carry for you.

It is so hard to say goodbye.

I gave you my love, my soul,

all the joy I ever had.

Someone like you will never again

walk into my life the same way.

You made me lift my head,

smile even through the pain.

I would drive across cities,

across the state,

just to see you once more.

My love for you cannot be taken away.

The good times and the bad,

the anger, the sadness,

every moment we lived

will always remain one truth,

one love, one way.

Looking So Good to Me

Why can't I look into your eyes

and say what my heart feels?

Why do I run away from you

when all I want is to stay?

I never want to hurt your heart.

I do not know how to say no,

or how to ask you

to run away with me.

If I fall down,

if I hurt myself,

would you care?

If tears fall on my face,

would you still care?

I would love to walk with you,

if you say yes.

You are looking so good to me.

My world would become your world.

Everything I have

would be yours.

My love is real for me and you.

All the stars in the sky
would be yours to keep.
I would sail across the ocean for you,
walk across the land just to see you.

Tell me what your heart wants.
I will do my best to reach you.
My love will always be yours to keep.
The keys and the locks on my heart
will belong to you.

I am going to love you,
always.

You look so good to me,
all the time,
for life.

P.S.

I really do love you.

I Cry So Hard

I am thinking of you
walking, sleeping,
all the time.
I cry so hard.

You gave me the world
and even more than I could hold.
You gave me your love
and all the joy in my heart.
You never let me fall
without holding me close.

You told me you loved me
and would always be there.
I cry so hard
because you are not here anymore.

You cannot hold me now
or wipe the tears from my eyes.
I reach for you in every thought
and find only silence.
I cry so hard.

I cry for the joy you gave me,
for the smiles you left behind,

for every word that once lit my world.

I pray to God

that I will see you again,

that I will feel you near once more.

I walk and look around,

whispering to myself,

I miss you so much.

I cry so hard.

Someone told me

that happiness lives in the heart.

I will never let it go,

because my heart belongs to you.

I Am Your Heart and Soul

How can I show you

something you can truly feel?

If I place my love in your hands,

will you hold it,

or let it drift into the wind?

I want to know

if you really want me.

I search for answers,

ask so many questions.

You may look at me like I am crazy,

but tell me,

will you stay or not at all?

So I will tell you the truth about me.

I am your heart and soul.

I would give you half of my life,

just to see you believe in us.

And if I feel your love return,

that is when my heart

gives everything it has.

I will look up and say,

Thank you, God,

for the love you placed in my life.
Tears will fall from my eyes for you.
My love will always stay faithful.

The sky will stay blue.
The moon will always shine.
The grass will stay green for you.
The wind will move and whisper
this is real love in the air.

The water will be whatever you need it to be.
The birds will sing love songs for you.
And I will remain,
your heart and soul,
always.

You Left Me All Alone Again

I cry all the time without you.
I do not want to call
or talk to anyone about you.
My heart hurts so much,
and sadness keeps coming.

I do not want to hear your name.
I do not want anyone
telling me anything about you.
Please stay out of my life.
Let me sit somewhere and cry.

I hate you so much right now.
I tell myself
I will get over you someday.
I need you to stay away
so I can learn how to breathe again,
so I can learn to love myself again.

You left me all alone again.

But my love will not disappear.
It will go somewhere new,
to someone who wants to love me back.
If you ever look around,
you will see it too.

Someone out there

wants to love you for who you are.

Do not stop.

Do not let fear win.

Go forward and try again.

God says

He will give you someone

who will make you happy,

someone who will be true to you.

Love will come and go,

again and again.

So do not let good love

go to waste.

It Hurts So Much

I let the tears run down my face.

I think about all the happy times we had.

It hurts so much to say goodbye to you.

I cry because I wish it never happened at all.

Sometimes I turn around,

listening for you to speak.

The words you said,

the way you made me laugh,

they are still with me.

I will always miss the time we shared.

I miss holding your hand.

I walk around hoping the rain will fall on me.

Sometimes I wish you were still here with me,

so I could tell you how I feel.

I need the hugs and kisses

that only you could give.

Your words made me feel better about myself.

You never let me go too far.

You told me what was right

and what was wrong.

I still listen and hear your voice.

Even when I did not like it,

I now understand you were right.

Missing you still hurts so much.
I cry, wishing you were beside me.
I try not to fall on my face,
and when I do,
I feel you helping me back up,
telling me to try again,
to try harder.

I hope to see you someday in heaven.

Please do not cry for me,
because God did not make a mistake with me.

Please do not cry for me,
because your love will be there forever.

Please do not cry for me,
because I am in heaven, waiting for you.

Please do not cry for me,
because your loving heart will always remain.

Please do not cry for me.
God told me we will see each other again.

So if you come to see me,
I will be there at the gate,
waiting and laughing,
telling everyone our story,
about you and me.

Do not let the tears keep falling.
We will see each other again.
And if you cry for me,
know this is true.

I will always love you more.

Mom, Don't Cry Anymore

Mom, don't cry anymore,
God gave you all the love you poured into me.
I am still here, carrying your lessons,
and your love stays with me every day.

You gave me everything I needed,
and all your children still love you.
You believed in me,
prayed for me,
and shared both my joy and my pain.

You were the love I needed every day,
the one who guided me when I lost my way.
Even when I stumbled,
your love showed me the right path.

Mom, don't cry anymore,
because I am waiting for you in heaven to
smile.

God promises we will meet,
and our hearts will rejoice together.
So wipe your tears,
and remember the love we shared.

You are my best mom,
and I will always love you.

I Am a Real Soldier

I am a real soldier,

always standing on your side.

I fight beside you,

catch you when you fall,

and lift you back to your feet.

I wipe the tears from your eyes

and walk with you through every storm.

If we fall, we fall together.

If we rise, we rise as one.

No one can hurt us when our hearts are joined.

I will show the world

that love like ours is real.

I am your soldier,

and I will not let anyone harm you.

With sword in hand and shield raised high,

I stand around you, guarding your heart.

You are my queen,

the one I choose to protect and love.

God made this world,

and in it, He gave me you.

So you will not have to cry,

or fear the hands that try to wound you.

I am the first in line for you,

and I will be the last to leave.

I will love you always.

The world will see us,

you and me, standing together.

You are my world,

my chosen love,

and no one will take that from us.

My soul, my heart,

my mind and body

belong to you.

Loving someone is not easy.

Letting go is even harder.

I Miss You Too

I am crying for you now.

It hurts so much not to see you anymore.

The sadness keeps coming,

and my world will never feel the same again.

The rain falls with cold air around me,

and I think of the beautiful smile you gave me.

I miss you more than words can say.

I miss having you to say hello to,

to ask how I am doing,

to say goodbye and tell me to be good.

You were the one who made my days brighter.

Now I cry and whisper that I miss you.

I told you so many times how much you meant to me,

and I loved every moment of it.

Now there is so much I want to say,

but I cannot,

because you are no longer here with me.

Until We Meet Again

I will pray to God.
Someday, we will see each other again.
Until then, my sunshine, you still light up my life,
and I hope the tears will stop running down my face.

This time, I will tell you how I truly feel about you.
I ask for the good times of your love
to find their way back to me again.

Please, sign the application.
I want you to be the one who reads this letter
and places your name upon it.
This is something I must know.
Do you really want me, or not?

If you are real, then say yes.
If your heart feels this too, then show it.
This application is the only way I know how to ask,
and I believe you want this as much as I do.

Sign the application only.
If you do this for me,
I will give you all my love.
My time will always belong to you.
My world will become about you and me.

Everyone will see our love shining through my life.
We will walk through the garden together,
smiling as the flowers smile back at us.
The green grass will whisper how sweet love can be.
The sky will stretch above us, blue and full of color.

I hope you are the one
who signed it.

You Are My Queen

Can you tell me what a Queen is?

She is a woman loved deeply,
a woman held with honor.
She is someone you look up to,
someone you protect with care.

A Queen is treated with respect,
in words, in actions, every day.
She may be a mother,
a sister,
an aunt,
a friend,
or the one your heart belongs to.

So I ask you now,
are you my Queen?

If you are, I will stand for you.
I will walk beside you and guard your peace.
No harm will reach you while I am near.
If you cry, your tears will not fall unnoticed.
I will catch them gently and hold them close.

I will build a home around your dreams,

a place where you feel safe and seen.

Let the world know who you are to me.

I am devoted,

and you are my Queen.

I will give you all that I have,

my time, my loyalty, my heart.

Not gold or silver alone,

but love that is true and lasting.

You are my Queen,

and my love for you is real.

www.ingramcontent.com/pod-product-compliance
Lightning Source LLC
Chambersburg PA
CBHW040115150726

48005CB00013B/1712